BIG MACHINES

Diggers

David and Penny Glover

W
FRANKLIN WATTS
LONDON•SYDNEY

This edition 2008

Franklin Watts
338 Euston Road, London, NW1 3BH

Franklin Watts Australia
Level 17/207 Kent Street, Sydney, NSW 2000

Copyright © Franklin Watts 2004

Series editor: Sarah Peutrill
Designer: Richard Langford
Art director: Jonathan Hair
Illustrator: Ian Thompson
Reading consultant: Margaret Perkins, Institute of Education, University of Reading
Picture credits: Jonathan Blair/Corbis: 6. Franklin Watts: 12t. JCB Ltd: 11c, 15b, 20, 21. Courtesy of
Komatsu Ltd: front cover, 4, 8, 12b, 14, 15t, 22. Courtesy of Orenstein-Koppel GmbH: 23. James A.
Sugar/Corbis: 10. Courtesy of Volvo Construction Equipment Ltd: 7b, 9t, 9b, 16, 17b, 18t, 18b, 19.
Woodmansterne/Picturepoint/Topham: 7t. Every attempt has been made to clear copyright. Should
there be any inadvertent omission, please apply to the publisher for rectification.

With particular thanks to Komatsu and Volvo Contruction for permission to use their photographs.

A CIP catalogue record for this book is available from the British Library.

Dewey number: 629.225
ISBN: 978 0 7496 7810 4

Printed in Malaysia

Franklin Watts is a division of Hachette Children's Books, an Hachette Livre UK company.

Contents

Digging holes

Diggers are big digging machines. They dig deep holes and long trenches on building sites. Diggers are also called excavators.

Pipes   **Trench**   ▲ This digger is digging a trench for underground pipes. The pipes are laid in the trench, then covered over again with soil.

Diggers sometimes do other work too. This digger is clearing rubbish from the sea.

BIG FACT

A big digger can do more in a day than hundreds of people working with picks and shovels.

The bucket

A digger picks up a load in its bucket. The bucket is made from strong metal so that it does not bend or break as it lifts.

Bucket

◄ This digger's bucket is picking up soil.

The bucket is shaped
so that it scoops up
soil as it turns on
the end of the
digger's arm.

The bucket has
sharp teeth to
cut into soil or
even rock.

Teeth

Grabs and grapples

A digger doesn't just dig holes. The driver can change the bucket and fit a grab or a grapple to do different jobs.

A grab is useful for loading a pile of soil or stones onto a truck.

A grab has two halves that bite together like a mouth.

A grapple has four or five curved spikes like long teeth. It is useful for picking up big rocks in a quarry, or rubbish at a dump.

Grapple

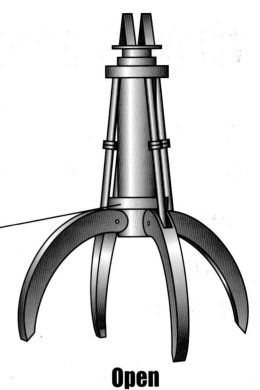

Open

As the driver raises the grapple the spikes close, hooking onto the load.

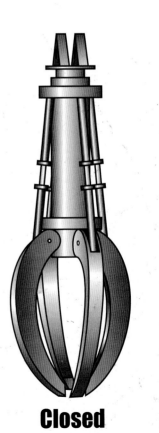

Closed

The boom

The digger's long arm is called the boom. It swings and bends to move the bucket just where it is needed. The boom has joints like a human arm.

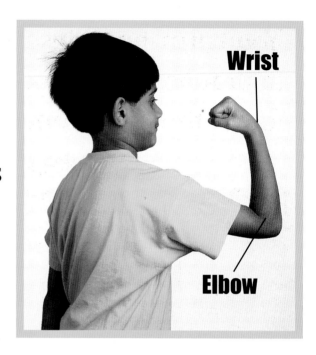

Wrist

Elbow

Hydraulic ram   Cylinder   Piston

KOMATSU

PC 290 NLC

KOMATSU

Boom   Joint A   Joint B

Joint A works like an elbow to bend or straighten the boom.

Joint B works like a wrist. It turns the bucket to scoop up and release the load.

Your arm has muscles. A boom has hydraulic rams. Hydraulic rams make the forces that bend and straighten the joints.

Hydraulic ram

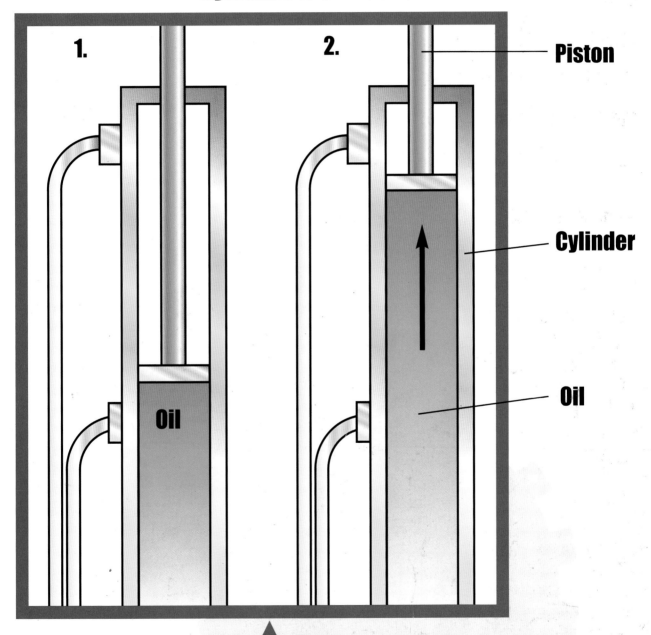

1.

2.

— Piston

Cylinder

Oil

Oil

Oil fills the cylinder, pushing the piston up.

Tracks and wheels

Some diggers move around on tracks.

Tracks give a good grip on rough ground. They stop the digger slipping as it scoops up its load.

Diggers with tracks can work on steep slopes. ▶

Tracks

Each track is a loop of metal links.

Other diggers have wheels. When a wheeled digger is working it must put down legs to stop it from slipping or tipping over.

Link

Legs

The engine

The engine is the part of a machine that makes it go.

A big diesel engine powers a digger.

Engine

When it is working a big excavator uses a litre of fuel every minute.

The driver fills the fuel tank with diesel. The diesel burns inside the engine, making hot gases. These gases make the engine work.

Engine

The fuel tank on this small digger is under the driver's steps.

▼

Step   **Fuel tank**   **Fuel tank cap**

Digger controls

The digger driver sits inside the cab. Buttons and levers work the different parts of the machine.

Cab

Two joysticks work the boom and bucket. It takes a lot of practice to drive a digger well.

Track controls

Joysticks

A digger with tracks does not have a steering wheel like a car. Two levers change the speed of the tracks.

Straight ahead

Same speed

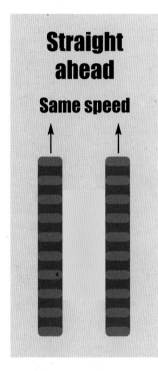

Turning left

Slower   Faster

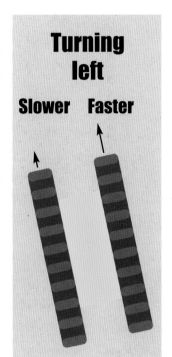

Turning right

Faster   Slower

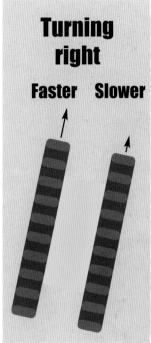

When both tracks move at the same speed the digger goes in a straight line. When one track goes faster than the other, the digger turns.

Cab turning

The driver can turn the cab around to move the arm to a new place. The digger picks up a load, then swings it round to the back of a truck.

Mini-excavator

Sometimes a digging job must be done in a small space, such as a back garden. Then a mini-excavator is used.

Boom

Bucket

Tracks

This digger is about the size of a small car. But it has just the same parts as the huge diggers used on large building sites.

Mini-excavators can drive through a narrow gap between two houses, or turn around in a small room.

This mini-excavator is using a drill to break up a concrete floor.

Giant diggers

Giant diggers work in quarries and mines. They dig out rocks from huge holes in the ground. The rocks may contain metals and other materials.

▲ This digger uses the teeth in its giant bucket to break off the rock.

This is the biggest digger in the world. Its job is to dig up sand in Canada. The sand contains oil. The digger is called the RH400. It could pick up an ordinary road digger in its gigantic bucket.

BIG FACT

The RH400 is so big it has a rest room for the crew. This has a microwave oven, a water dispenser, a coffee machine, a refrigerator and beds.

The RH400 standing next to a normal-size digger.

Make it yourself

Make a model digger.

You will need:

Paints

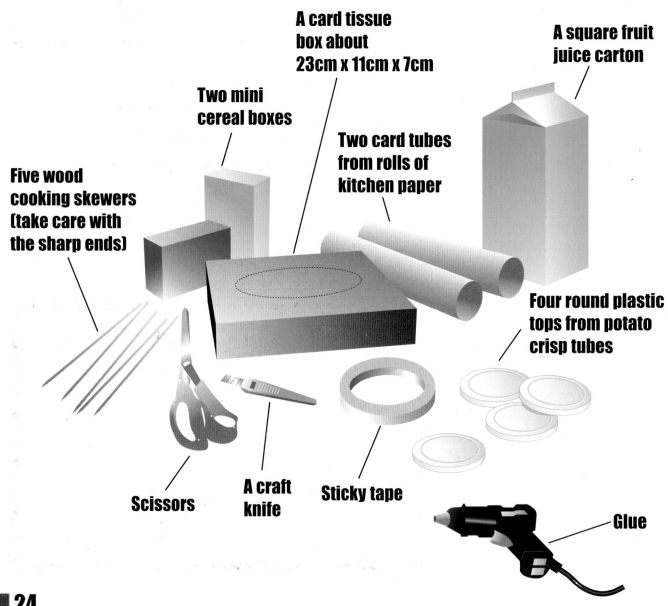

A card tissue box about 23cm x 11cm x 7cm

A square fruit juice carton

Two mini cereal boxes

Two card tubes from rolls of kitchen paper

Five wood cooking skewers (take care with the sharp ends)

Four round plastic tops from potato crisp tubes

Scissors

A craft knife

Sticky tape

Glue

SAFETY! An adult must help you with the cutting and sticking.

1. Glue the cereal boxes to the tissue box to make the digger body and cab. Cut a slot about 6cm x 6cm at the front of the digger body.

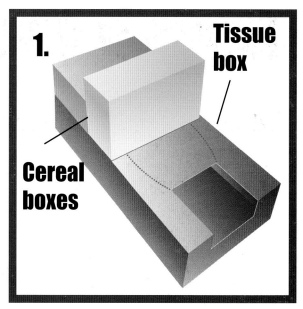

2. Cut two pieces about 5cm x 4cm from one end of a card tube as shown.

Make holes in the tabs.

3. Make small holes in the second card tube. Push the skewer through both tubes as shown. Trim the skewer to length.

This is your digger's boom.

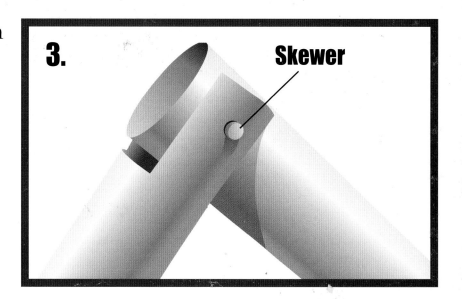

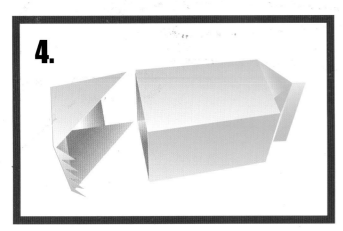

4. Cut the base from the fruit juice carton. Use scissors to shape it into a digger bucket. Don't forget to make the teeth!

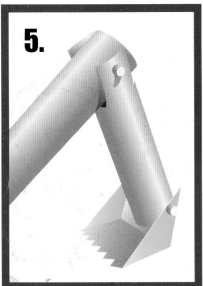

5. Attach the bucket to one end of the boom with a wooden skewer.

6. Use another skewer to fix the other end of the boom in place in the digger body.

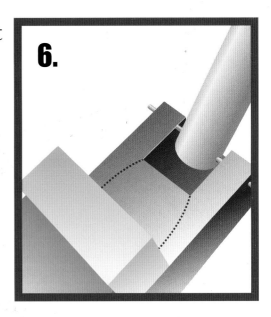

7. Push two skewers through the digger body from one side to the other to make axles.

Make holes in the round tops and push them onto the axles to make wheels. Trim the axles.

Move your digger bucket by bending the boom at its joints. Scoop up a load.

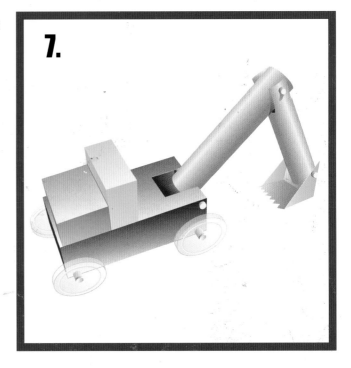

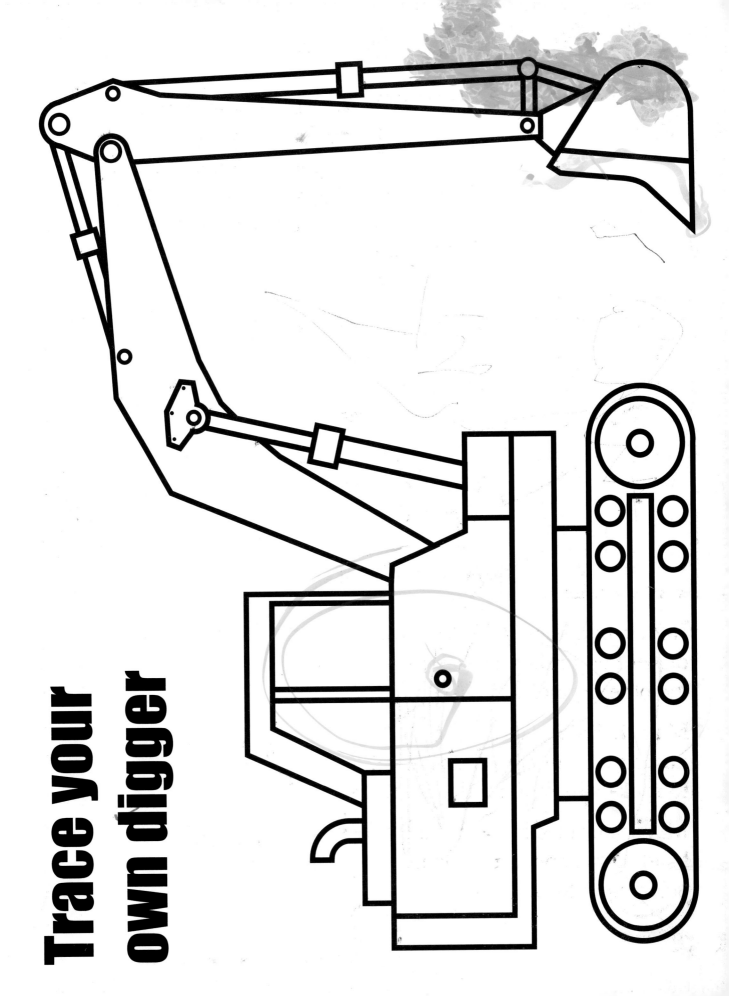

Trace your own digger

Digger words

boom

The digger's arm. The boom has joints, like an arm, that bend as the digger works.

bucket

The heavy scoop on the end of the boom. The bucket has sharp teeth to cut into soil or rock.

cab

The part of a digger in which the driver sits.

diesel

The fuel the digger engine uses to make it go.

engine

The part of a machine that burns fuel to make the forces that turn its wheels and move its parts.

excavator

Another name for a digger.

grab

A tool like a big mouth that can pick up loads of sand and soil. A grab can be fitted to the digger in place of the bucket.

grapple

A tool made of curved spikes that can pick up large rocks and pieces of metal. A grapple can be fitted to the digger in place of the bucket.

hydraulic ram

The part that pushes to bend the boom or turn the bucket. The ram is worked by oil, which pushes a piston along a cylinder.

joystick

A control like a lever for moving the boom or bucket.

tracks

The loops of metal links that some diggers have instead of wheels.

Index